Fly Your Dreams Today

Fly Your Dreams Today

Life Begins When You Do

Wa Leopard

PARTRIDGE

ISBN: Softcover   978-1-4828-7653-6
               eBook   978-1-4828-7652-9

To order additional copies of this book, contact
Toll Free 0800 990 914 (South Africa)
+44 20 3014 3997 (outside South Africa)
orders.africa@partridgepublishing.com

www.partridgepublishing.com/africa

CONTENTS

When it rains, most birds head for the shelter,
The Eagle is the only bird that in order to avoid rain, starts flying above the cloud.
Like a bird in flight, your life can soar above the troubles of the world.

DEDICATION

This book is a special dedication to my darling mum who taught me that life is a journey that begins with a single step and no matter the hard times better times are yet to come tomorrow. Never to give up on hope. She is my hero *"Shujaa"*.

My mum taught me to live your life to the fullest potential, and fight for my Dreams.

Begin – Never Quit – Whatever you can do, or dream you can, begin it. Boldness has genius, power and magic in It, Begin Now! You are never too old to set another goal or dream a new dream.

Mum advised that a man can be as great as he wants to be. If you believe in yourself, have the courage, determination, dedication, and the competitive drive. If you learn from defeat, then you haven't really lost.

If you are willing to sacrifice the little things in life to pay the price for the things that are worthwhile, it can be done.

Believe it can be done. When you believe, something can be done, really believe, your mind will find the ways to do it. Believing a solution paves, the way to solution. The world is but a canvas to our imagination?

If you wait for the perfect moment when it is all safe and assured, it may never arrive. You must move mountains.

Whatever you can imagine, you can accomplish. The canvas of life awaits you. The painter of your dreams. Fly your own Dreams Today.

INTRODUCTION

After hitting the rock bottom, I read a copy of Napoleon Hill Book Think and Grow Rich the secret to a successful life was born. It inspired me to motivate other people who feel that they want to give up in life. If you learn from defeat, you haven't really lost.

When defeat comes, accept it as a signal that your plans are not sound, rebuild those plans, and set sail once more toward your coveted goal."

"Before success comes in any man's life, he is sure to meet with much temporary defeat, and, perhaps, some failure. When defeat overtakes a man, the easiest and most logical thing to do is to quit. That is exactly what most men do. More than five hundred of the most successful men America has ever known told the author their greatest success was realized just one step beyond the point at which defeat had overtaken them.

Whatever the mind can conceive and believe it can achieve. Every choice you make has a result. If you want to achieve greatness stop asking for permission. You are the master of your destiny. You can influence, direct and control your own environment. You can make your life the way you want it to be. A goal properly set is halfway reached. If you want to reach a goal, you must "see the reaching" in your mind before you arriving at your goal.

My business ran down due to tough economic conditions; I was bankrupt most of the so called "friends" disappeared on me. I was denied some privileges since other people had "close ties" with the authority in power. Then I got sick and was taken for surgery but after overcoming all this I decided it was my time to motivate many people who might be going through rough times to develop success from failures.

I decided to turn my life around and the weapon I used was a pen and paper to put all my shortfalls to create strength to other people. There is a saying that says "Your business is never really good or bad out there", your business is either good or bad between your own ears". This book is to encourage people who are struggling not give up on their dreams. "Your dream is valid" Lupita Nyongo Oscar Award Winner.

It is never too late, just wake up and work on your dreams. Start today you have nothing to lose. But you have the whole life to win. "Today's pain is tomorrow's power, the more you suffer today the stronger you are tomorrow.

Dreams are illustrations from the book your soul is writing about you. Keep calm and live your dreams.

Self-pity is self-defeating. Tomorrow's success is based on today's discomfort, plus willpower is like a muscle, the more you exercise it, the stronger you will get.

The worst words you can say are "I just wish I had" Push yourself to do what you hope to do so you will never have to regret not having tried.

Follow your dreams they know the way.

Recognize that you have all the greatest of men have had. Know where you are weakest and where you are strongest and improve both. Become better every day. The distance between your dream and reality is called action. All our dreams can come true if we have the courage to pursue them. Take a chance.

The coward dies a thousand deaths, but the brave warrior dies once. Dive in cold water it's never as cold, or as bad as you think.

Bravery means finding something more important than fear. Brave people aren't fearless, they've simply found something that matters more than the fear they're facing.

Find a reason that has great meaning than fear; your desire to make a difference; your family's future or your dream of a more fulfilling life.

You must do it or not. There is no trial. Persistence matters don't say I'll try say I will and keep the promise to yourself.

And the easier it is to call on when dedication and persistence makes all the difference. If you can visualize it, you can dream it, there is some way you can do it.

In real life experience always turn the negative situations into positive I believe that's the best revenge. You will get all you want in life if you help enough other people get what they want. "Stop selling. Start helping". The key to success is keeping company with people who uplift you, whose presence calls forth your best. Find good mentorship and counsellors that challenge you to change. Express your love and respect to people who mean the world to you.

Take good care of people that take care of you. Become better every day. Discover the power of your subconscious mind to bring health, wealth and happiness to your life.

Like the way, a farmer turns the animal waste to manure and grows crop to produce a bumper harvest. We should take our past failures as lessons for the future. Lack of direction and not lack of time is the major problem.

We have twenty-four hours' day. Remember that failure is an event not a person.

Yesterday ended last night. Develop success from failures, discouragement and failures are two of the surest stepping stones to success.

Like the athlete who set achievable goals to win the marathon, keeps on practicing hard enough and really works towards achieving the goal, when eventually they close the tape to be the world Champions there are so excited of their great achievement that they forget of their exhaustion.

The best dreams happen when you are awake. Stop waiting for the right time. Time is now. Talent, experience and connections are important but they grow with time. Never give up on a dream just because of the time it'll take to accomplish it. The time will pass away anyway.

I admire people who choose to shine after the storms they have been through. The extra mile is a vast, unpopulated wasteland. Discover your purpose and dedicate your life to fulfilling it. Remember that failure is an event, not a person. Yesterday ended last night. If you don't see yourself a winner, then you cannot perform as a winner.

Summary

Chapter 1 – Beyond Positive Thinking

Your unlimited power lies in your ability to control your thoughts. A confused mind works in the direction of sickness, poverty, lack and limitation rather than in the direction of abundance, health and success. The only way we can truly heal the world is to heal ourselves first. We need to remind ourselves of *who we are* and what we are capable of. We need to take responsibility for everything that has happened to us. Thought leads to feelings, feelings lead to action, action leads to results.

Your financial situation can only grow in the same pace as you grow. If you must change the fruit, you must change the roots. If you want to change the visible, you should change the invisible first. Money is a result, riches are a result, health is a result and weight is a result. We live in a world of cause and effect.

Chapter 2 – The future Belongs to those who belief in the Beauty of their Dreams

Every Great Dream Begins with a dreamer. Have visions work hard towards the dreams until you fulfil it. Become a dreamer find the way to the universe until the dream is realised then make your dreams happen. All your dreams will be realised when you follow them.

Forget the past, follow your dreams, cherish a beautiful vision and walk gently through the world and realise its beauty, wait and enjoy the better things in life and live a happy fulfilled life.

Cherish your dreams and your vision they are the blue print of your ultimate achievements. Man, should have a dream in life and realise it. Believe in the beauty of your dreams, they are given to you for a reason.

As soon as you start to pursue a dream, your life wakes up and everything has a meaning. The future belongs to those who believe in the beauty of their dreams. Think big, Believe Big, and the outcome is **HUGE!**

Chapter 3 – SERENITY – Peace comes from Within You

Serenity is inner peace within the storm. Create a peaceful moment from all life handles. Be calm in times of chaos. When you become still and lose your mind in nature you will become still and find a doorway to a new world.

A calm heart finds peace within. You allow miracles to happen to yourself and become like a shade-giving tree in a thirsty land or a sheltering rock.

We all love a tranquil mind and peaceful life. It does not matter whether it rains or shines by being in the nature is always serene and calm.

Discover yourself in nature leave only your footprints but discover your soul and the beauty of the wilderness and the calmness of the humble places of mother nature, for the world's beauty is truly amazing.

You are Your Own Creator "You Become What You Think About"

Chapter 4 – Self Confidence

Whatever you expect, with confidence, becomes your self-fulfilling prophecy. When you confidently expect good things to happen, good things always happen to you. If on the other hand, you anticipate negative things to happen, you are usually not disappointed.

Wealthy people expect to be rich. Successful and popular people expect to be happy and popular. Expect the best in yourself.

Imagine that you have unlimited abilities and you can accomplish anything you set your mind.

Your future is only limited to your own imagination, and that whatever you have accomplished up to now, is only a fraction of what you are truly capable of achieving.

Imagine that the great moments lie ahead and everything that has happened to you up to now has merely been a preparation for the great things that are to come.

Confidence is the **POWER** that determines your uniqueness, your talents, your background, and your experiences have all culminated to make you, an original work of art and knowing that you belong. Confidence is a natural expression of ability, expertise and self-regard. "Those who believe they can do something and those who believe they can't are both right"

Affirm your own value as a human being today; affirm the value of your life purpose and your chosen projects and the commitment of seeing your projects through to complete.

Visualize and see yourself living the life you desire, doing things you want and being the person you want to become. Life isn't about finding you but about creating yourself. Start living now. Every day you are alive is a special occasion. Every minute, every breath, is a gift from God.

Chapter 5 – Motivation

"*Motivation is what gets you started. Habit is what keeps you going*". Jim Ryun

How to stay motivated: - Take one day at a time. Surround yourself with positivity. Create a dream board. Ask yourself what you want and make realistic goals accordingly. Reward yourself, belief in yourself; acknowledge your attitudes recognizing your progress.

Visualize accomplishing your goals and be kind to yourself and don't compare yourself with others. Face your past without regrets, Handle the present with confidence, Prepare the future without Fear, Keep the faith and drop the fear, The past is a lesson; the present is the gift and the future a **motivation**.

Think about the achievements in your life. Begin writing your life purpose. Examine your strengths to understand what you can build on. Determine what other people see as your strengths and key capabilities. Set achievable goals for yourself, work to achieve them, and enjoy that achievement.

You may have to fight a battle more than once to win it.

Good things come to people who wait, but better things come to those who go out and get it. If you do what you always did, you'll get what you always get.

Thinking should become your capital asset, no matter whatever ups and downs you come across in your life.

Think empowering, expansive thoughts. It is our choices that show what we truly are, far more than our abilities. You establish your real priorities in life by choices of how you allocate your time.

Chapter 6 – Success

Believe you can succeed and you will. The size of your success is determined by the size of your belief. Create and pursue focused goal. Focus on being productive and not being busy.

Success is to be measured not so much by the position that one has reached in life, as by the obstacles which he has overcome. Strong lives are motivated by dynamic purposes. Success comes from taking the initiative and following up... persisting... eloquently expressing the depth of your love. Success is in direct proportion to our service.

Success is not the result of making money, earning money is the result of success. "Don't concern yourself with money, Be of service ..., build..., work..., dream & create. Do this and you'll find there is not a limit to the prosperity and abundance that will come to you.

You may only succeed if you desire succeeding; "We become what we think about most of the time, and that's the strangest secret."

The first step towards success is taken when you refuse to be a captive of the environment in which you first find yourself. Successful people take decisive and immediate action; they make logical and informed decisions, and work outside the comfort zone. They act as if it's impossible to fail. Success is the sum of small efforts, repeated day-in and day-out.

"As You Plant –So you shall reap". Plant the seed into your mind, care for it, and work steadily towards your goal, it'll become a reality. Each must live off the fruits of our thoughts in the future; we are guided by our thoughts. We become what we think about. Start Today. You have nothing to lose. But you have the whole life to win. Courage is resistance to fear, mastery of fear - not absence of fear. Keep an eye on the goal and keep moving towards the target.

Coming together is a beginning, keeping together is a progress and working together is success. Success is liking yourself, liking what you do, and liking how you do it. Your unlimited power lies in your ability to control your thoughts.

A confused mind works in the direction of sickness, poverty, lack and limitation. A successful man looks at the direction of abundance, health and success. if you want to make a permanent change, stop focusing on the size of your problems and start focusing on the size of you.

Chapter 7 – Success and Failure

Success is failure turned inside out. - I can accept failure; everyone fails at something. But I can't accept not trying." Success is walking from failure to failure with no loss of enthusiasm." Winston Churchill.

Success is not final; failure is not fatal. It is the **courage** *to* continue that counts. The difference between a successful person and others is not lack of strength, not lack of knowledge but rather lack of willpower. Success is about creating benefit for all and enjoying the process. If you focus on this and adopt this definition, success is yours, success is limitless.

To succeed your desire should be greater than your failure. Success is how high you bounce when you hit bottom.

Develop success from failures. If success is to be yours, you can rest assured that you're going to have to work at it. To be the best, you must give your best; you should work harder than the rest. While people are resting, you must be working. Success is a game, you must play hard, you should out-smart the competition, and you should put in the work.

Always believe that if you put in the work, the results will come. "I don't know the key to success, but the key to failure is trying to please everyone."

Never fear failure, fear not trying, fear not giving your best, fear losing focus, but never fear failure. Failure is the path to success. Failure is the sign that you're headed in the right direction. To succeed twice as fast, fail twice as much.

Fail often, fail daily, and soon you will succeed. Never be afraid of failure it's the stepping stone to success.

Ultimately, success is all about taking your shot, repeatedly. Sometimes you may win, sometimes you will lose, but the more things you try, the more chances you have of succeeding. Put the power of numbers on your side. Take as many shots as you can. There's no guarantee of success, but when you don't take a shot, there's a definite guarantee of failure.

Chapter 8 – The Power of Gratitude

Gratitude makes sense of our past, brings peace to today, and creates a vision for tomorrow.

With gratitude, all the life appears to be a blessing, without gratitude all of life is perceived as a burden.

Being grateful for the blessings you get in your life, including the life lessons that come from setbacks; sets your mind for positive thinking and for enjoying a positive life.

Count your Blessings: -

Gratitude unlocks the fullness of life: -

It turns what we have into enough, and more. It turns denial into acceptance, chaos into order, and confusion into clarity.

It turns a meal into a feast, a house into a home, a stranger into a friend. The way of happiness is "Zero-Based Gratitude".

Focus on what you have, you'll be happy and you'll feel good about yourself, not miserable on what you don't have.

Be grateful not only for others but for yourself. Visualize a great future; holding on a mental image of a great future is the first step to creating that future.

Let us be grateful for the people who make us happy. They are charming gardeners who make our souls blossom. The smallest thanks are always worth more than the effort it takes to give it.

To feel good about yourself, you must trust yourself. Trust your purpose, trust your goals, trust your abilities and trust your inherent worth as a person. Gratitude is a powerful process for shifting your energy and bringing more of what you want in life. Be grateful for what you already have and you will attract more **Good Things**.

The more you Thank Life the more life gives you to be thankful for.

Appreciate what you have right now, no matter how little it seems in comparison to what others have. This is one of the most powerful secrets to adding riches to your life. When I started counting my blessing, my whole life turned around. Develop an "**attitude of gratitude**" toward whatever you have now and watch how it will begin to grow and increase. *He who can give thanks for little will always find he has enough. Acknowledging the good that you already have in your life is the foundation for all abundance.*

CHAPTER 1

Beyond Positive Thinking

Don't let the fear of losing be greater than the excitement of winning.
Robert Kiyosaki

Build your own self-image. Deliver your creativity to the masses. Meditate and visualize success daily and realize your thoughts become your reality. You must "see" yourself in your picture. Deliberate affirmation or self-talk, combined with visualization, produces the result. Embrace excellence in everything we do.

As we continue to do it repeatedly, soon our subconscious accepts that it is true for us. The real key here is in not trying to be different from your picture.

Modify the picture first. Real growth and change begins from the inside out. We must first change the picture in our mind. As we do this, our comfort zone will expand automatically.

This becomes our new truth. We then act in accordance with that new truth or belief. Have faith in your ability to succeed. Get into action today.

People without money feel victimized, but what they don't understand is that they live a self-fulfilling prophecy. Therefore, the rich get richer and the poor get poorer. It has nothing to do with money. People with winning self-images cause themselves to do things that win. If they lose occasionally, they don't accept it as their fate. Instead of working on our actions, we want to work on our self-image.

Work on our self-talk begins in any given area we choose to change. We start to control our self-talk so that when us behaviour is other than what we want it to be, we will say to ourselves in some manner, "That's not the way I am. That's not like me." Then make an affirmation as to what "Me" is like,

"It's like me to be a winner." "It's like me to be loving." "It's like me to be successful." "It's like me being an author."

When I do something that is successful, something that in the past would not have been like me, I must then, through my self-talk, reinforce my belief by saying, "That's the way I am." "That's like the new me." "I am successful, easy to get along with, outgoing, etc. As I do that, the subconscious records my self-talk. It does not record what is happening; it records my *opinion* of what is happening. What I image to be true is what I record.

Your unlimited power lies in your ability to control your thoughts. A confused mind works in the direction of sickness, poverty, lack and limitation rather than in the direction of abundance, health and success. The only way we can truly heal the world is to heal ourselves first. We need to remind ourselves of *who we are* and what we are capable of. We need to take responsibility for everything that has happened to us. Thought leads to feelings, feelings lead to action, action leads to results.

Your financial situation can only grow in the same pace as you grow. If you must change the fruit, you must change the roots. If you want to change the visible, you must change the invisible first. Money is a result, riches are a result, health is a result and weight is a result. We live in a world of cause and effect. Rich people associate with positive successful people; poor people associate with negative unsuccessful people. Keep your eye on the goal, and keep moving towards your target. This is not a new message, but I think we need to remind ourselves of *who we are* and what we are capable of. We need to take responsibility for everything that has happened to us Through the law of attraction, we attract either consciously or unconsciously everything that happens to us.

Whatever anyone has done to us, we have participated in it, and are at some level, responsible. There are no victims, only volunteers. This is a hard pill to swallow, but unless we accept it we cannot change things for the better. We have become a culture of blamers.

The secret of success is not to try to avoid, remove or escape from problems; the secret of success is to become bigger than your problems. The purpose of our lives is to add value to the people of this generation and those to follow. Your field of focus determines what you find in life.

Your life is important. It is important to you, and it is important to the rest of the people on this planet. I believe that every person on this planet arrived here with a mission.

If you will listen to your intuition your purpose or your mission will be revealed to you. We established our purpose, build our vision and set our goals. Your goal should be something you dearly want; it should be your heart desire. Its helping you move in the direction of your vision.

Your vision was established with a long-term view of doing the thing you love to do, having BIG DREAMS with definite plans for carrying out their desire. That's what turns Dreams into Goals.

Dr Ben said I am a good neurosurgeon by acknowledging that's a gift from God but to excel with using my gifted hands, I went for training and sharpening of my skills. One of my goals is to make sure that teenagers learn about highly talented individuals so that they can have a variety of role models to enable them change their attitude and set their sights towards higher achievements. We encourage the youth to look at themselves as God-given talents. We all have abilities. Success in life revolves around recognizing and using raw materials.

TO THINK BIG and use of our talents doesn't mean they are no problems or obstacles along the way. How we view these obstacles determine how we end up.

If we choose to see the obstacles as barriers we stop trying. If we choose to see the obstacles as hurdles we can reap over them. Success people are determined that no obstacles will stop them.

Whatever direction we choose, if we can realize that every hurdle we jump strengthens and prepares us for the next one, we're on the way to success.

Life is like a Drama

When you do not understand why people act as they do, try to see life as a drama in which the actors and actresses are following a written script with monotonous precision, never questioning their parts.

If heartache is written into the scene, heartache will always be there if the players follow the script. But life is not a fixed drama. It only appears so because we don't question the roles that we are playing. The way to change the role is to change the script, and you can rewrite the script if you don't like the part.

Kindly note that nothing, nor anyone who can stop us from creating the life that we desire. **The only one who can ultimately stop us is ourselves and our own limited beliefs**. Decide right now that you are open, responsive and receptive to new ideas and beliefs that will support you in getting to where you want to go and that you are willing to give up anything that limits you in any way.

Take up one idea, make the idea your life, think of it, dream of it, and live on that idea. Let the brain, muscles, nerves and every part of your body be full of that idea and just leave every other idea alone. This is the way to success.

When you hold the image of your goal on the screen of your mind in the present sense, you are vibrating in harmony in resonance with every particle of energy necessary for manifestation of your image in physical plane. By holding that image those particles of energy are moving towards you (attraction) and you are moving towards them- because that the Law. **Law of Attraction.** All things are merely manifestations of energy or spirit.

When the world comes to understand this great truth, we will be aware that all people are the same. The true diving lines are not colour or language, but simply ignorance and it opposite understanding. Know the truth and the truth will set you free.

Allow yourself to take the next step right now. A step that goes Beyond Positive Thinking!

CHAPTER 2

The Future belongs to those who Believe in the Future of their Dreams

DREAM! BELIEVE! SUCCEED! – IF YOU CAN DREAM IT YOU CAN DO IT! Walt Disney

Dream Big! Believe Big!

Go confidently to the direction of your dreams. Start today to be successful, be positive don't fear failure it's the stepping stone to success.

Write every single day in your life, write what should not be forgotten. All you must do is to write your heart out. You're putting it down to the world you are expressing your inner beliefs.

I get my inspiration by writing a motivational book "FLY YOUR DREAMS TODAY.

It gives me strength by believing that it will create a positive impact to the readers by motivating them never to give up in their dreams. Let your dreams become the children of your soul and the blue print of your ultimate achievements.

A writer will always tell a story even when there is no hope or promises, he will express his soul until no tale is left to tell. A writer will always will always write like it matters and eventually it will matter when after writing a blog, a book becomes a part of him. A writer can be inspired by anything either a failure or success. By picking the pen and paper or typing on the keyboard of the computer he will tell a tale that can change the world, he should write what will not be forgotten by the reader. He creates an impact to the word by the stroke of his pen.

Even if he fails again and again to accomplish his purpose, the strength of character gained will be the measure to his true success. This will form a new starting point for future power and triumph. Let your dreams be bigger than your fears and actions louder than your words. All our dreams can come true if we have the courage to pursue them.

Winners never quit and Quitters Never Win. If you never chase your dreams you will never catch them! If you remain true to your dreams, your world will at last be built. Purpose, energy, power to do and all strong thoughts cease when doubt and fear creep in. Doubt and fear are the greatest enemies of knowledge.

He who has conquered doubt and fear has conquered failure. It is better to fail originally than to succeed in imitation.

All that a man achieves and all that he fails to achieves is the direct result of his own thoughts. There can be no achievements or progress without sacrifice. And a man's success is measured by strengthening his resolution and self-reliance.

Fortune sides with him who dares. Little minds are tamed and subdued by misfortune, but great minds rise above it. Real difficulties can be overcome; it is only imaginary ones that are unconquerable. Failure is the condiment that gives success its flavour. Positive thoughts yield positive result and negative thoughts yield negative result. "You sow what you plant". All achievements are governed by positive directed thoughts.

A man can only conquer and achieve by lifting his thoughts. He can only remain weak and miserable by refusing to uplift his thoughts.

If you think positive the greater will be your success, and the more blessed and enduring will be his achievement. The universe does not favour the greedy, the dishonest, and the viscous. Intellectual achievements are realized after the search for knowledge or for the beautiful and true in nature.

The dreamers are savours of the world. Dream lofty dreams and as you dream, so you shall become.

Composer, painter, poet are makers of the after-world, the architects of heaven.

He who cherishes a beautiful vision, a lofty idea in his heart, will one day realize it.

Columbus cherished the vision of another world and he discovered, Bill gates discovered Computer software Windows, Safaricom Ltd in Kenya discovered MPESA-mobile money transfer and it's getting better each day.

Each day is a new canvas to paint upon. Make sure your picture is full of life and happiness, and at the end of the day you don't look at it and wish you had painted something different. Look at everything as though you were seeing it either for the first or last time Only WISE MEN whose thoughts are controlled and purified makes the winds and storms of the soul obey him. Just like planting the good grain you will surely realize a bumper harvest.

Good thoughts and actions bear good fruits or good results. You become what you think about. Immerse yourself with the right thoughts and you will become the person you long to be. Then your time on earth will be filled with glory.

Every great dream begins with a dreamer. Always remember, you have with you the strength, the patience, and the passion to reach the stars and change the world. The successful warrior is the average man, with laser-like focus.

"Start with big dreams and make life worth living."—Stephen Richards

All our dreams can come true if we have the courage to pursue them.

Cherish your visions, cherish your ideas and cherish the music that stirs your heart, the beauty that forms in your mind, the loveliness that drapes in your purest thoughts.

For out of them, will grow all delight conditions all heavenly environment; off these, if you remain but true to them your world will be at last built.

Take up one idea, make that one idea your life, think of it, dream of it, and live on that idea. Let the brain, muscles, every part of your body be full of the idea, and just leave every other idea alone, this is the way to success.

Example - Kenya's Javelin Legend Julius Yego - how watching YouTube videos of javelin throwing inspired and motivated him to Winning Gold in the World Championship.

Chase the dream; sometimes sprint after it, sometimes you just walk, sometimes you even stop to catch your breath. Just don't quit on it or yourself.

If you genuinely want something, don't wait for it, go get it and teach yourself to be patient. The whole secret of a successful life is to find out what is one's destiny to do, then do it.

Every day is a new beginning - a day for a new plan and new action.

If today, in conscious awareness, you choose the same plan as yesterday, you are wise. If you choose a different plan, you are equally wise. Whatever you choose, choose with intention. Let your light shine. Fulfil the promise that is within you Choose to soar.

Choose to fly your dreams. Begin Today put your dreams into Action.

Dream This Day of Wondrous Things, of Peace and Hope and Pride. Dream Big and Achieve, Work Hard, Stay Focused & Surround Yourself with Good people, conspire to aspire before you expire.

The desire is to obtain; to aspire is to achieve; "Ask and you shall be given". Your vision is the promise of what you shall one day be your ideal is the prophecy of what you shall at last unveil. The greatest achievement was at first and at a time a dream.

Dreams are seedlings of realities. The vision that you glorify in your mind, the ideas that you enthrone in your heart, this will build your life by this you will become.

If you want to make a permanent change, stop focusing on the size of your problems and start focusing on the size of you. The best revenge is massive success. Anyone who keeps the ability to see beauty never grows old. Life is full of beauty. Notice it. Smell the rain, and feel the wind. Live your life to the fullest potential, and fight for your dreams.

Though we travel the world over to find the beautiful, we must carry it with us or we will find it not.

It is not the magnitude of our actions, but the amount of love that is put into them that matters. Whenever you see a successful person you only see the public glories, never the private sacrifices to reach them.

Everyone has inside of him a piece of good news. The good news is that you don't know how great you can be if you work hard towards your goal what you can really accomplish the power is within you tap it now. The scariest moment is always before you start.

Just don't quiet on the dream and yourself. Dream big, work hard, stay focused and surround yourself with good people. Don't waste on people who deserve your silence.

Sometimes the most powerful thing you can say is nothing at all. Powerful dreams inspire powerful action. When you can taste, smell and touch your dream you can enrol the world. Life is either a daring adventure or nothing. Security is mostly a superstition; it does not exist in nature. Every day is a day to act.

Whatever your choices, act on those choices: **Today is your day to spread, Wings and soar, Fly life on free wings, and Sing to its glory.**

Follow what you are genuinely passionate about and let that guide you to your destination. A good plan is like a roadmap and the courage into your destination.

Destination is not a matter of choice, it is not something to be waited for but rather it's meant to be achieved. One's destination is never a place but rather a new way of looking at things.

Breath deep, choose and break the shackles of your past. Don't wait, Do it today, and again tomorrow. Today is your day of going an extra mile. Start today you have nothing to lose, but you have the whole life to win.

> *Yes, I am a dreamer, for a dreamer is the one who find his way by moonlight, and see dawn before the rest of the world.*

All your dreams will come true when you have the courage to pursue them. Always follow your dreams, be of service to people, have a purpose and money will be the result. In the end, you'll live a Life You Have Always Dreamt About.

CHAPTER 3

SERENITY - Peace comes from within. Do not seek it without.

Each one must find his peace from within. And to be real must be unaffected by outside circumstances.

Serenity is peace within the storm. Inner peace is realised the moment you control your emotions, you are like a calm clear sea after the storm. Serenity bestows inner peace, tranquillity and calmness of mind.

The quieter you become, the more you can hear, go into the wild forest lose your mind and find your soul in the silence of trees swaying.

In the forests, you experience silence where the earth write's the music of your soul. After spending a day in the wilderness or in the ocean nature's beauty stirs the heart, inspires imagination and brings out eternal joy to the soul.

Make your own happiness and peace of mind a priority. Try to find calm in the chaos, find peace in your heart.

Serenity comes by trading expectations for acceptance. Be strong enough to stand alone, smart enough to know when you need help and brave enough to ask for it. Serenity isn't the absence of conflict but the ability to cope with it. It is the tranquil balance of heart and mind.

God, give us the grace to accept with serenity the things that we cannot change, courage to change the things that can be changed and wisdom to distinguish the difference. Let every step we make, every step we take can be filled with peace, joy and tranquillity.

Serenity is peace realised amidst a storm but not freedom from storm. The fruit of silence is tranquillity. Serenity yields happiness in life since the creative achievement is realised at the tranquil time. He is like a sheltering rock in storm.

Only the wise man, only he whose thoughts are controlled and purified makes the wind and the storms to obey him. Self-control is strength. Right thought is mastery. Calmness is power. Immerse yourself in the thoughts and you become the person you long to be.

Nothing gives one person so much advantage over another as to remain always cool and unruffled under all circumstances. Do not look for happiness outside yourself. The awakened seek happiness inside. Inner peace can be reached only when we practice forgiveness. Forgiveness is letting go of the past, and is therefore the means for correcting our misperceptions.

You were born a child of light's wonderful secret you return to the beauty you have always been. The reality is that peace can only be found within. Peace is not a new job, or a new car, peace is a new perspective, and that new peace begins with you. To be at peace is to be during noise, trouble but manage to be calm in your heart and work harder. At the beginning of each project visualize what success will look like. If the project is writing a new book, visualize your title as listed as a no. 1 best seller list. Make it a habit practice to recall this image of success every day. Pleasure is always derived from something outside you, whereas joy arises from within.

Solitude is priceless –look for peace and tranquillity
- Solitude is the secret of geniuses, and the master key of personal success.
- The ideas you need to succeed are only born if you are still and quiet. I love solitude, the doorway to solitude opens when you have nothing to do, and
- nowhere to go without, so you are forced to travel within.
- In solitude, in stillness and in quiet, is when mind is free to ponder what has been
- keeping you from making significant progress. In solitude, the steps required to move you forward are revealed. Everything significant in my life has been conceived in stillness and contemplative silence.

Serenity is the last lesson of Culture: -
Serenity is the flowering of life, the fruitage of soul; it is precious as wisdom and more desirable than fine gold. How insignificant mere money-seeking looks in comparison with a serene life. A life that dwells in the ocean of truth, beneath the waves; beyond the reach of tempest, in the external calm.

"Underneath the Ocean below the waves lies a beautiful paradise". In the ocean of life, the isles of blessedness are smiling and the sunny shore of your ideal awaits your coming. Keep your hands firmly upon the helm of thought. In the core of your soul reclines the commanding master, he does not sleep wake him. Self-control is strength, right thought is mastery, and calmness is power say unto your heart; PEACE! BE STILL!

Thoughts are creative.

Your thoughts are the primary creative forces in your life. The word proactively **means more than merely taking initiative**. It means that as human beings, we are responsible for our own lives. Our behaviour is a function of our decisions, not our conditions. We can subordinate feelings to values. We have the initiative and the responsibility to make things happen.

Proactive people can carry their own weather with them.

Whether it rains or shines makes no difference to them. They are value driven; and if their value is to produce good quality work, it isn't a function of whether the weather is conducive to it or not. *No one can hurt you without your consent.*

"They cannot take away our self-respect if we do not give it to them." It is our willing permission, our consent to what happens to us, that hurts us far more than what happens to us in the first place.

Make the right choice and a person can say deeply and honestly, I am what I am today because of the choices I made yesterday.

It's not what happens to us that hurts most, things can hurt us physically or economically and can cause sorrow, but our response to what happens to us that hurts us.

We should learn to develop the personal freedom in difficult circumstances to lift and inspire others and motivate them to more noble acts of service and compassion. You create the entire world by the way you think.

All the people and situations of your life have been created by your own thinking, and when you change your thinking positively, you change your life can sometimes change in seconds. It is not the world outside you that dictates your circumstances or conditions it is the world inside you that creates the conditions in your life.

The most important principle of personal or business success is simply this: -

"You become what you think about most of the time".

Accurate diagnosis is half then cure. Specifically, it is the way you think about money and your financial situation that largely determines your financial conditions today. **As a man thinketh, "As you think, that is what you become."**

For when you expect something wonderful to happen, that is watching and praying without ceasing.

When you are not feeling up to par physically or our mind is becoming clouded with doubt, we should realize it is time to pray with more conviction on work at developing a stronger feeling of expectation. You must guard your mind constantly against doubt, because it is crippling vibration.

The instant you become aware you are entertaining thoughts which create doubt become quiet, start relaxing and imagine yourself already in possession of prosperity you desire. When you do this, you are altering the mental current which is flowing into your marvellous mind. Expect, with all your conscious, to receive your good in your material world. You think in secret and it comes to pass, environment is but you're looking glass.

Expect good result that's what you will receive. What you see is what you get.

Steps of achieving prosperity in life: -

1. Build an image in your mind, turn over to spirit – (**Let Go and Let God**).
2. Expect with your **heart & soul** that spirit will reward you openly for your faith.
3. **Expect Abundance**
4. **The Law of Vibration and Attraction**

   Any idea that is held in mind that is either feared or reverend will begin at once to cloth itself in the most convenient appropriate physical form available. The body is the servant of mind, whether they be deliberately chosen or automatically expressed. In case of beautiful thoughts, the body is clothed with youthfulness and beauty. Strong pure and happy thoughts build up the body in vigour and grace.

   A strong body, a bright happy and serene environment can only result when you let in air and sunshine freely in your rooms. The aged who have lived a righteous calm, peaceful and softly mellowed like a setting sun. By wishing everyone well, be cheerful to all and finding the positive in people will bring you eternal peace.

   Projects that exist only in your mind are unlikely ever to be completed. Begin writing down your life purpose; write down your projects that support the intent of the thread. Half of finishing a project is beginning – and most of the rest is never quitting. Very little in life is complex. Begin and keep going. If necessary, begin again each day.

Know that you can only fail if you quit.
   What you believe in is what you get. It's better to conquer yourself than win a thousand battles, and then the victory will be yours. It cannot be taken from you; not by angels nor demons, heaven or hell.

He who conquers himself is greater than the mighty. To conquer yourself you must conquer your mind. You must control your thinking. Dismiss thoughts that are constantly to the life you desire to live. It's a man's own mind, not his enemy or foe that lures him to evil ways.

There is always something to be grateful for, recognize it and give thanks. A grateful heart will make you great. Let us rise and be thankful at least we learned a little, we didn't get sick, or didn't die. So, lets us all be grateful for the breath in us.

Reflect upon your present blessings of which everyman has many not on your past misfortunes, of which all men have some. Your life reflects your thoughts. If you change you're thinking. You change your life but if your thoughts are negative, the world will see it the same.

Celebrate your victories: - whenever you complete a project have a huge celebration. Even if you haven't meant your goals celebrate. Always celebrate what you have learned. Celebrate learning what works and what doesn't work.

It is necessary then, to cultivate the habit of being grateful for every good thing that comes to you, and give thanks continuously because all things have contributed to your advancement.

Use support Network- if you have friends and family who support your life purpose, include them in your projects. Let them be keepers of your time frames and milestones include them in celebrations and your painful life lessons.

Join organizations that are compatible with your life purpose and seek support. Also, make conscious decisions to spend less time with people who don't support your goals and life purpose.

Everything in life reflects a choice you have made. If you want a different result, make a different choice. For when you want something wonderful to happen, that is watching and praying without easing. When your mind becomes clouded with doubt, you should guard your mind constantly against and doubt, because it's a crippling vibration.

Start having positive thought and imagine yourself already in possession of prosperity you desire. Expect good results and that's what you will receive. "What you see is what you receive". Build an image in your mind, turn it over to spirit.

Expect with your heart and soul that spirit will reward you openly for your faith.

Travel well today, enjoy the journey. Life is about the journey. I am not trying to arrive; I am already there. I am happy and content and satisfied where I am today. I may experience nicer places, finer wines but I am traveling well.

Don't put off your happiness into some nebulous time in the future based on some goal that you think will bring you happiness. It's better to travel well than arrive.

Expect Abundance. –

Abundance is simply believing in your own magic. You attract abundance by visualising what you desire and belief its already there. Manifest your desires by giving them attention, intent and emotion. Feel grateful in everything, that works out perfectly when you trust the universe it gives exactly what we need. Everything you hold in your conscious thought becomes your cage and reality.

Your soul will leave a life of your dreams by seeing and creating abundance, embracing good and being honest. Be a living magnet by believing in your dreams and the universe will serve it. You attract what you want y being your own creator. You the power, courage and strength, compassion and love to become what you want to be. Be a success story creating a life that you have always imagined.

By having positive thoughts and believe you can achieve the impossible you will realize the life you have always wanted, doors will start opening and you will have the universe in your palms. Expect miracles by attracting what you believe you deserve.

The best belief that you can develop within yourself is that you are destined to be a big success financially and in life. When you are absolutely convinced that you are a financial success in the making, you will engage in the behaviours that will make it come true. The worst you can have are "self-limiting beliefs". These exist whenever you believe yourself to be limited in some way.

Whatsoever anyone else has done, within reason, you can probably do as well. You just need to know how. Opportunities don't happen, you create them.

Plant seeds of happiness, hope, success, and love; it will all come back to you in abundance. This is the law of nature.

If you always attach positive emotions to the things you want, and never attach negative emotions to the things you don't, then that which you desire most will invariably come your way. We are the music makers, and we are the dreamers of dreams.

We cannot control the wind, but we can direct the sail. A dream written down becomes a goal. A goal broken down into steps becomes a plan and a plan backed by Action makes you realise your dream. Remember you are never too old to set another goal or dream a new dream.

Chapter 4

SELF CONFIDENCE – Life is a climb but the view on top is worth it.

Low self-confidence isn't a life sentence. Self-confidence can be learned, practiced, and mastered just like any other skill. Once you master it, everything in your life will change for the better. Self-confidence is the only exit, from your present season.

Self-confidence should be celebrated for your uniqueness. You must have confidence in YOU!

Self-confident person is admired by others and inspire confidence in them. He faces his fears head-on and tends to be risk takers. He knows that no matter what obstacles come his way, he can get past them. Self-confident person tends to see his live-in a positive light even when things aren't going so well, and he is typically satisfied with and respect himself.

Whatever you expect, with confidence, becomes your self-fulfilling prophecy. When you confidently expect good things to happen, good things always happen to you. If on the other hand, you anticipate negative things to happen, you are usually not disappointed.

Wealthy people expect to be rich. Successful and popular people expect to be happy and popular. Expect the best in yourself.

Imagine that you have unlimited abilities and you can accomplish anything you set your mind.

Your future is only limited to your own imagination, and that whatever you have accomplished up to now, is only a fraction of what you are truly capable of achieving. Imagine that the great moments lie ahead and everything that has happened to you up to now has merely been a preparation for the great things that are to come.

Confidence is the **POWER** that determines your uniqueness, your talents, your background, and your experiences have all culminated to make you, an original work of art and knowing that you belong.

Confidence is a natural expression of ability, expertise and self-regard.

Those who believe they can do something and those who believe they can't are both right.

Effective ways to promote your own self-confidence.

1. Think and act positively

Positive energy leads to positive outcomes, so set your mind to the can-do side of any situation, avoiding the negative self-talk that can make you feel less confident. Smile, laugh and surround yourself with happy, positive people. This is the time to really evaluate your inner circle, including friends and family. This is a tough one, but it's time to seriously consider getting away from those individuals who put you down and shred your confidence.

You'll feel better and the people with whom you work will enjoy your company.

Be positive, even if you're not feeling it quite yet. Put some positive enthusiasm into your interactions with others and hit the ground running, excited to begin your next project. Stop focusing on the problems in your life and instead begin to focus on solutions and making positive changes.

2. Be the change you want to realize

Change your mind and body. The body achieves what the mind conceives. Set small goals and build upon them.

By exercising not only do you become physically fit and your health improves but it changes the mind, your attitude and your mood. The body is because of the choices we make, your body can stand almost anything, it's your mind that you must convince. Progress is impossible without change.

By staying positive and changing your brain and the way you see things, your body begins enjoying no matter whatever the shape, age, size or fitness level.

Your body is a slave of the mind. Nothing can be achieved without being enthusiastic. Change your mind and change your life. You'll feel good about your body and your own self. By changing your mind and building confidence you start the process of healing your body.

When our minds change, our behaviour changes the outcome.

The only thing standing between you and your goal is yourself. Be the change you want to realise, the difference between an ordinary and *extra ordinary* person is going the extra mile.

3. Act the Part.

There's more to being confident than just how you look. You must act the part.

Practice being self-confident and soon it will become second nature. Inaction breeds doubt and fear, while action breeds confidence and courage. As an exercise, jot down your strengths and weaknesses. Most people will tell you to work on your weaknesses, but use what you've got and capitalize on your strengths instead. Once you put more energy into your positive traits, your confidence will start to shine through.

4. Proper planning promotes pea performance

A goal without a proper plan is just wishful thinking.

Spectacular achievement will always be proceeded by spectacular preparation and proper preparation prevents poor performance.

When you plan a daily schedule, you'll experience the level of confidence and with time become more competent. Before a task is started the leader should plan and provide a purpose, direction and motivation to his followers so that they can work confidently towards accomplishing its mission.

Planning or being prepared is half victory, when you plan for a lifetime you train as well as educate people to perform and stand out from the crowd. Good plans that are organised shape up good decisions, hence planning makes your dreams come true.

5. For tough times, when all else fails: Create a *great* list and avoid negativity

Life is full of challenges and there are times when it's difficult to keep our self-confidence up. Low self-confidence is often caused by the negative thoughts running through our minds on an endless track. If you are constantly bashing yourself and saying you're not good enough, aren't attractive enough, aren't smart enough or athletic enough, and on and on, you are creating a self-fulfilling prophecy.

You are becoming what you are preaching inside your head, and that's not good.

Never give up. Never accept failure. There is a solution to everything, so why would you want to throw in the towel? Make this your new mantra.

Succeeding through great adversity is a huge confidence booster. Low self-confidence is often caused by the negative thoughts running through our minds on an endless track.

If you are constantly bashing yourself and saying you're not good enough, aren't attractive enough, aren't smart enough or athletic enough, and on and on, you are creating a self-fulfilling prophecy. You are becoming what you are preaching inside your head, and that's not good. The next time you hear that negativity in your head, switch it immediately to a positive affirmation and keep it up until it hits the calibre of a self-confidence boost.

6. Speak assertively.

The next time you listen to your favourite speaker, be mindful of the way he or she delivers a speech. A great speaker speaks confidently, in a steady, rhythmic tone. Adopt an assertive, but not aggressive, way of speaking that indicates your self-confidence. You will feel your self-esteem begin to rise. To be taken seriously, avoid high-pitched, nervous chatter or twittering giggles in your speech. People will listen to you more attentively when they see the leader radiate from within you.

You are a living magnet; you invariably attract into your life the people, situations and circumstances that are in harmony with your dominant thoughts.

When you develop a burning desire for financial success and think about it all the time, you set up a force field of positive emotional energy that attracts people, ideas and opportunities into your life to help make your goals into realities.

Take full credit for all good things in your life. They are there because you have attracted them to yourself. Affirm your own value as a human being today; affirm the value of your life purpose and your chosen projects and the commitment of seeing your projects through to complete.

Visualize and see yourself living the life you desire, doing things you want and being the person you want to become.

> *The world has enough beautiful mountains and meadows, spectacular skies and serene lakes. It has enough lush forests, flowered fields, and sandy beaches. It has plenty of stars and the promise of a new sunrise and sunset every day. What the world needs more of are people who will appreciate and enjoy it."*
> *"Happiness is part of who we are. Joy is the feeling"*

Pause to appreciate the beauty around you. Whether rainbow or butterfly, mountain or tree, painting or poem; whether crafted by nature or by a human hand, beauty adds a magical element to life that surpasses logic and science. Life isn't about finding you but about creating yourself. Start living now. Stop saving the good china for that special occasion. Stop withholding your love until that special person materializes. Every day you are alive is a special occasion.

Every minute, every breath, is a gift from God.

Focus on your inner beauty "Though we travel the world over to find beautiful, we must carry with us or we find it not. True beauty is in the inside.

Choose to spend more time with those who appreciate you. To feel good about yourself be kind and compassionate to others.

Be of service to others. The wise man does not lay up his treasures. The more he gives to others, the more he has his own.

Release all anger, resentments and hatred. *Holding onto anger is like gasping a hot coal with the intent of throwing it to someone else".*

To feel good about yourself choose to release all anger and resent by forgiving everyone for everything. Forget justice and forget revenge. Give yourself the gift of forgiveness so you can feel better about yourself.

Positive thoughts yield positive life and negative thoughts breed's negative circumstances. Learn to feel good about yourself.

Live a joyful and stress-free life, feel better about yourself, Love your life.

When you say that you are not feeling good enough the fact is that you are responding to hostile critic from your family and friends or comparing yourself with other people. You are responsible for your own goals and aspiration for your life, as well as your thoughts, your own choices and your actions. Be your own self. **"Always be a first-rate version of yourself instead of a second-rate version of someone else."**

Set your life purpose, establish your values, make your own choices, and begin your own projects. Allocate your time, energy, money and emotional commitment as you choose. Trust your own value system, you can please everyone, you will make yourself miserable if you try.

Define your own life purpose, trust yourself, trust your values, and trust your actions you take in support of these values.

"Have no regrets -forgive yourself" God grant me the serenity to accept things I cannot change, Courage to change things I can and wisdom to know the difference.

To feel good about yourself, you must forgive yourself for everything you have ever done or failed to do.

Wipe the slate clean -erase all your regrets. Let today be a new beginning for the rest of your life.

Care for your body, whatever size or physical abilities, love yourself as you are. You will feel better about yourself when you take care of yourself the best way possible. Eat healthy, get enough sleep, avoid stress, start healthy practices.

Care for your mind. Think depressing thoughts and you'll be unhappy. Think positive thoughts and you'll be happy. Avoid stressful thoughts since stress is harmful to your mind and your body as well as your emotional state. Begin daily practices to support your mental and emotional health, inspiration reading and meditation. Righteousness not corruption, is the moulding and moving force in the spiritual government of the world.

Watch your thoughts, for they become words, watch your words, for they become action. Watch your actions, for they become habits. Watch your habits, for they become character. Watch your character, for they become destiny.

Care for your spirit. You'll feel better about yourself if you see a purpose to your life beyond the present moment. Whether from a religious or philosophical perspective, look beyond today with optimism for your future and that of human kind.

The qualities of truly confident people are: -

1. Truly confident people aren't afraid to be proven wrong. They feel finding out what is right is more important than being right and admit to their mistakes when they are wrong.
2. Truly confident people listen ten times more than they speak. They are quiet and unassuming; they already know what they think but will require your opinion. They ask what you do, how you do it, what you like about it, and what you have learned from it. They know the only way to learn more is to listen more. They are very observant.
3. Truly confident people don't need the glory, **they know what they have achieved, they don't need validation of others because true validation comes from within,** so they stand back and celebrate their accomplishments through others. They stand back and let others shine a confidence boost to the others too.
4. Confident people are secure enough to ask for help from others simply because they need assistance and want to pay a huge compliment to the person assisting.
5. Truly confident people know that access is almost universal. They connect with everyone through social media, choose the path they wish to follow by attracting their own funding, build networks and create products. They follow whatever course they wish to go out and do it.
6. Truly confident people don't put down other people. They are the person they were yesterday and the person they hope to become in future.
7. Truly confident people aren't afraid to look silly. They don't mind occasionally being in a situation where you aren't at your best. Oddly enough people tend to respect you more when you do -not less.
8. Truly confident people own their mistakes. Confidence breads sincerity, honesty, truly confident admit mistakes. They dine out on their screw-ups. When you are truly

confident, you admit occasionally "looking bad". You realize that when you're genuine and unpretentious, people don't laugh at you, they laugh with you.

They only seek approval from people who really matter. Confident people earn trust and respect of the few people in your life that truly matter. When you earn their trust and respect, no matter where we go or what we try, we do it with true confidence, because we know the people who truly matter the most are truly behind us.

If you really want to do something, you'll find a way. If you don't find an excuse you are responsible for how you feel no matter what someone does to you.

Remember you are in control of your thoughts so choose to feel confident and adequate rather than angry and insecure. Life is full of give and take. Give thanks and take nothing for granted. No matter who tries to bring you down, hold my head high and get up every time. Self-confidence is the most attractive quality a person can have. Difficult doesn't mean impossible it simply means you must work hard. Think highly of yourself and people will respect you bring yourself down people will downgrade you.

The best project you'll ever work on is you. Decide to thrive not just survive. **FEAR** has two meanings: - "***Forget everything and Run***" or "**Face everything and Rise**" the choice is yours. Stay positive, tomorrow will be amazing.

Self-confidence destroys doubt, intimidates your enemies, and inspires your friends. When you're confident, you know that there's nobody like you.

Be authentic by gaining an inner recognition of you, know what makes you unique.

Self-confidence has everything to do with the future that you create for yourself.

Self-confidence is not arrogance but an inner recognition of your greatness.

Life is the most difficult exam. Many people fail because they lake confidence in themselves and copy others, not realizing that everyone has a different question paper.

The greatest gift you can give to somebody is your own personal development. I used to say if you will take care of me, I will take care of you, now I say take care of me for you. When you love, yourself you can transfer the love to others.

How to Gain Self Confidence & Build Self Esteem: -

> "*Those who believe they can do something and those who believe they can't are both right*". Henry Ford

1. **Choose your battles**
   Match your talents with your goals. If you are trained to be an accountant don't search for a nurse job it'll end up harming your self-confidence.

2. **Build on success**

    Create small success first later build a hierarchy upon that success to gain self-confidence and move on to a larger accomplishments and success.

3. **Be objective**

    Have a realistic assessment on what you can or can't do by knowing your limitations is not an obstacle to self-confidence but rather enhances self-confidence.

4. **Expect some failures**

    Failures are part of life. If you don't fail you don't learn. If you don't learn you'll never change. Remember that failure is success in progress.

5. **Be persistent**

    Know your objectives, they are the directions and commitments that are meant to mobilise the resources and energies to achieve the planned goal. Have the determination and patience as you work towards success.

6. **Celebrate each victory**

    Make time to celebrate your accomplishments, no matter how big or small, remember success is the sum of small efforts repeated day in day out. Its fine to celebrate success but it is more important to heed lessons of failure.

7. **Find your life purpose**

    Trust your own Value system. He who has a why to live can bear almost anyhow. Find your life purpose and give your whole heart and soul to it.

    Live the life of your dreams per your vision and purpose instead of expectations and opinions of others. Let your passion lead you to your life purpose.

8. **Ignore Critics**

    Listen to the right people and ignore the critics. People who doubt you, hate you and judge you are never worth your time or attention. Ignore all the hatred and critics. Live for what you believe and do what you perceive to be right.

    Don't let the noise of other opinions drown out your inner voice. Have the courage to follow your heart and intuition they already know what they anticipate to become.

9. **Associate with positive people**

    Surround yourself with people who will only lift you higher. It's better to be alone than in bad company. Choose the company you keep carefully.

You become the 5 people you mostly spend your time with. Surround yourself with good, intelligent, kind hearted, positive and loving people. People who make you happy make it easier to build your self-esteem since they respect you and support your life purpose and goals.

10. **Do not Compare Yourself with others.**
   Stay Focused on your own journey and leave footprints behind
   Your only obligation in any lifetime is to be true to yourself. The only person you should try to be better than is the person you were yesterday.
   Never compare yourself with others you have no idea what their journey was all about. Remember we all have our unique abilities given by the Almighty they are good in one thing i.e. an athlete but you are also gifted in another way i.e. a writer. Self-confidence is measured by our own unique needs.
   It's simply your own life to do whatever you choose.

11. **Answer to higher authority**:
   Believe in God and yourself. You are doing better than you think you are.
   Be about ten time more magnanimous than you believe yourself capable of and your life will be a hundred-time better off.
   The man who moves a mountain begins by carrying away smaller stones.
   Where there is hope, there is faith, where there is faith miracles happen.
   The strongest factors of success is self-esteem: - believing you can do it, believing you deserve it, believing you will get it and believing you are greater than your obstacles.

How self-confidence and self-esteem reinforce each other.

   Trust yourself and you'll know how to live.
   Self-confidence is how you feel about yourself. When you love, yourself you have a healthy self-esteem which makes you more confident.
   Self -esteem and self-confidence work best together.
   Confidence is silent, insecurities are loud. People who feel good about themselves are more likely to have confidence to try new opportunities.
   Building esteem is a first step towards your happiness and a better life.
   High self-esteem increases your confidence.
   Life changing secrets to boost your self-esteem.

   • Focusing on the positive & use of the affirmation
   • Have some solitary time -meditation & get a live coach and finally
   • Believing that things will get better.

By building both self-confidence and self-esteem you can live joyful and productively regardless of the circumstances.

Powerful ways to Boost Your Confidence: -

1. **Be positive even when you are not feeling like it**.
   Stop focusing on your problems but focus on the solutions and making positive changes. If you want to make a permanent change, stop focusing on the size of your problems and start focusing on the size of you.

2. **Know your strengths and weaknesses**
   Life is full of challenges and there are times when it's difficult to keep our self-confidence up. Believe in yourself, confidence may bring success but gives power to face any challenges. Make a list of all the things in your life that you are thankful for, what you have accomplished. Post it on a wall by your desk, or on somewhere where you can easily be reminded of what an amazing life you have and what an amazing person you really are. When you look at those lists your self-confidence is boosted and let yourself feel inspired all over again.

3. **Stay away from negativity and bring on the positivity by staying cheerful with a positive look of live**.
   Wherever you go, no matter what the weather, always bring your own sunshine. Evaluate your inner circle, those include your friends and family. Get away from people who put you down and shred your confidence.

4. **Change your body language and posture**.
   A simple act of pulling your shoulders back and walking straight up gives others the impression that you are a confident person. Smiling will make you feel better and others feel more confident around you. Your confidence is directly proportional to your success, and it is the secret to your success

5. **Work out**
   Along the same lines as personal appearance, physical fitness has a huge effect on self-confidence. If you're out of shape, you'll feel insecure, unattractive, and less energetic. By working out, you improve your physical appearance, energize yourself, and accomplish something positive. Having the discipline to work out not only makes you feel better, it creates positive momentum that you can build on the rest of the day.

6. **Focus on contribution**

Stop thinking about yourself and concentrate on the contribution you're making to the rest of the world, you won't worry as much about you own flaws. This will increase self-confidence and allow you to contribute with maximum efficiency. The more you contribute to the world the more you'll be rewarded with personal success and recognition.

CHAPTER 5

MOTIVATION – Motivation is what gets you started. Habit is what keeps you going.

Motivation is literally the desire to do things. It's the difference between waking up before dawn to pound the pavement and lazing around the house all day. It's the crucial element in setting and attaining goals—and research shows you can influence your own levels of motivation and self-control. So, figure out what you want, power through the pain period, and start being who you want to be.

How to stay motivated: -

1. Take one day at a time. Surround yourself with positivity. Create a dream board.   Ask yourself what you want and make realistic goals accordingly.
2. Reward yourself, belief in yourself; acknowledge your attitudes recognizing your progress.
3. Visualize accomplishing your goals and be kind to yourself and don't compare yourself with others.
4. Face your past without regrets, Handle the present with confidence, Prepare the future without fear, Keep the faith and drop the fear. The past is a lesson; the present is the gift and the future a motivation
   When you get motivated you can accomplish almost anything. I got motivated to write a book.
5. Always be a first-rate version of yourself instead of the second-rate version of somebody else. The only place where success comes before work is in the dictionary.
6. Think about the achievements in your life. Begin writing your life purpose. Examine your strengths to understand what you can build on. Determine what other people see as your strengths and key capabilities.

7. Set achievable goals for yourself, work to achieve them, and enjoy that achievement. You may have to fight a battle more than once to win it.

A goal properly set is halfway reached. If you want to reach a goal, you must "see the reaching" in your own mind before you arrive at your goal. When obstacles arise, you can change your direction to reach your goal, you don't change your decision to get there. You measure the size of your accomplishments by the obstacles you have overcome to reach your goal.

How to Get Motivated

Understand Your Life Purpose

A man can be as great as he wants to be. If you believe in yourself and have the courage, determination, dedication and the competitive drive. He becomes great if he is willing to sacrifice the little things that are worthwhile to achieve his life's purpose.

Until one has a clear idea of one's life purpose, there is no way to know whether a task is important or not.

Example of an author has a purpose of writing a book. Is writing this book important? Those questions can only be answered within the contents of one's life purpose. If a task isn't important to you, you can't motivate yourself to work on it consistently and energetically. However, more often the day-to-day activity (tasks) of your project doesn't seem rewarding, and only the result drives you. You want to become an author.

In these cases, it is crucial to find a means of visualizing the desired end-result daily and using the image of the desired result for daily motivation.:

Choose your priorities: -

It is our choices that indicate that we truly are for more than our abilities.

Be willing to leave your comfort zone.

The greatest barrier to achieving your potential is your comfort zone. Don't be afraid to make mistakes. Wisdom helps us avoid making mistakes and comes from making a million of them. Change your thoughts and change your world. It's by acts and not by ideas that people live.

Be miserable or motivate yourself.

Whatever must be done, it's always your choice and mostly don't let what you cannot do interfere with what you can do. You can do anything, but not everything. Good things come to people who wait, but better things come to those who go out and get it. If you do what you always did, you'll get what you always get. Thinking should become your capital asset, no matter whatever ups and downs you come across in your life. Think empowering, expansive thoughts. It is our choices that show what we truly are, far more than our abilities.

You establish your real priorities in life by choices of how you allocate your time.

Choose to undertake only projects that are compatible with your life purpose and choose to allocate majority of your time to tasks further to these projects.

At the beginning of each project i.e. writing a book, visualize your title listed as a number one bestseller book. See yourself excelling in what you anticipate to achieve.

Half of finishing a project is beginning –and most of rest is never quitting. Very little in life is complex. Begin and keep going. Know that you can only fail if you quit. Nothing is impossible: the word itself says I'm possible. The harder you work the more luck you'll seem to have.

Celebrate your victories whenever you complete a project even if you haven't met your goals celebrate. Choose to be happy. Happy people are easily motivated. Happiness is your birth right, so don't settle for anything else.

Happiness is not something you postpone for the future; it is something you design for the present.

When you are grateful, fear disappears and abundance appears.

Happiness is like a butterfly, which when pursued, is always beyond your grasp, but which, if you will sit down quietly, may alight upon you.

Beautiful things happen in your life when you distance yourself from the negative.

Spend at least one hour a day in self-development. Read good books or listen to inspiring tapes. Driving to and from work provides an excellent opportunity to listen to self-improvement tapes.

If you have family who support your life purpose includes them in your projects but don't spend time with people who don't support your projects.

A friend is someone who understands my past, believes in the future, and accepts me just the way I am.

The first step to success is taken when you refuse to be captive of the environment in which you find yourself. Give light and people will find the way.

There are two ways of spreading the light; to be the candle or the mirror that reflects it.

Train yourself to finish what you start. Finish one task before you begin another.

Put your heart, mind and soul into even the smallest acts, this is the secret to success Ideas shape the course of history. Live fully in the present moment. When you live in the past or the future you can make things happen in the present. Mankind is made great or little by its own will. The successful warrior is an average man, with laser-like focus.

Never quit when you experience a setback or frustration. Success could be just around the corner. It is during our darkest moments that we must focus to see the light. If you are willing to risk the usual, then you must settle for the ordinary.

Dare to dream big dreams. If there is anything to the law of expectation, then we are moving in the direction of our dreams, goals and expectations.

The real tragedy in life is not in how much we suffer, but rather in how much we miss, so don't miss a thing. We must be prepared, at any moment, to sacrifice who we are for who we can become. Judge each day not by the harvest you reap but by the seeds you plant.

Believe you can and you are halfway there. Leave a creative life by losing the fear of being wrong. Become the producer, director and actor in the unfolding story of your life by doing what we love and becoming cornerstone of having abundance in our life. There is no scarcity of opportunity to make a living at what you love; there's only scarcity of resolve to make it happen. Trust because you are willing to accept the risk, not because its right or certain.

Passion is the strong feeling of enthusiasm for doing something. Working hard for what you love to do is passion.

You get your true satisfaction by believing in what you are doing and by loving what you do your results become better and better as time passes by. When you love whatever, you are doing, you produce excellent results. When you choose a job, you love you'll never have to work a day in your life.

When you are, motivated or inspired to do the job, you love you'll never go wrong. Follow your passion by being prepared to work hard through sacrifice. Note the only great work is to love what you do.

Remember success is not achieved by working hard but working intensely and passionately.

There is no chance, no destiny, no fate that can hinder or control the firm resolve of a determined soul.

The most successful people in any society are those who take the longest time into consideration when making their day to day decisions. People at the highest social and economic levels make decisions and sacrifices that may pay off not for many years (a long time before they achieve it), sometimes not in their lifetimes.

You begin to move up socially and financially from the day you begin thinking about what you are doing in possible long-term consequences for your actions.

As you begin thinking long-term and organizing your financial life and priorities with your future goals and ambitions in mind, the quality of your decisions improves and your life starts to become better almost immediately. What seems to us as bitter trials are often blessings in disguise.

Your ability to practice self-mastery, self-control and self-denial to practice to sacrifice in the short term so that you can enjoy greater rewards in the long is the starting point of developing a long-time perspective.

People at the lowest levels of society have the shortest time perspectives. They focus primarily on immediate gratification and often engage in financial behaviours that are virtually guaranteed to lead to in debt, poverty and financial problems in long-term.

Self-discipline and sacrifice is the most important personal quality for assuring long-term success. When you continually invest your time and money in improving yourself rather than frittering it away by idle socializing or Watching TV, you are putting yourself on the **"Side of Angels"** You are virtually guaranteeing your future" when you stop chasing the wrong things and you give the right things a chance to catch you.

Move beyond your limits.

The limits can be overcome by moving beyond the impossible. We should look for opportunities by having the courage to face our limits, no matter how difficult the situation is.

We should not limit our challenge but challenge our limits by moving beyond them. We move beyond our limits when we pursue unrestricted areas and make the impossible become possible and achieve more goals is life making you becoming the best.

The only way of finding the limits of the possible is going above them into the impossible. We learn our limits by going beyond them and improving our weak points to become the perfect or a star in your field. We can only move beyond our limits when we accept our past mistakes and let them be our guide towards a brighter future.

Fear clouds opportunities, erases possibilities and limits to move beyond our current situation that is stuck. No matter how difficult the situation is we should move above it. Remember you can't put a limit on anything, the more you dream the more you work hard to realize your dreams and the better you become.

We can move beyond our comfort zone and you'll then realize it was never really that comfortable. Everything is possible when you put your mind, work and time into it.

Surround yourself with positive people who are higher than you. Associate with people who will uplift you for its better to be alone than in bad company. Choose your company carefully, you become five **"5"** people you spend most of your time with.

Surround yourself with people who make you happy, love you treat you right. When you meet various types of people from different cultures and backgrounds try learn from them since for the lesson learnt will uplift.

Do not spend your time with cynics or grumpy people. Life is too short to be nothing but happy. Respect yourself enough to walk away from the thing that makes you unhappy or stresses your life. Keep the company of like-minded people who were also positive and they will make you a better person.

Focus in the good in life, feel it, speak it and surround yourself with positive people who empower and encourage you. You are the product of your own environment. Surround yourself with people who genuinely care about you, they are the ones worth keeping in your life.

CHAPTER 6

SUCCESS – The size of your success is determined by the size of your belief.

You may only succeed if you desire succeeding; *"We become what we think about most of the time, and that's the strangest secret."*

Believe you can succeed and you will. Create and pursue focused goal. Focus on being productive and not being busy. Success is to be measured not so much by the position that one has reached in life, as by the obstacles which he has overcome. Strong lives are motivated by dynamic purposes.

Success comes from taking the initiative and following up... persisting... eloquently expressing the depth of your love. Success is in direct proportion to our service. Success is not the result of making money, earning money is the result of success.

Don't concern yourself with money, be of service, build, work, dream & create.

Do this and you'll find there is not a limit to the prosperity and abundance that will come to you. Don't worry if it brings fear and its crippling. If it fails for the first 30 days, go 30 more days repeat again and again each time it'll become part of you and you'll wonder if you could have lived any other way. MONEY! Yeas lots of it. But what's more important you'll have peace., you'll be in wonderful minority who lead calm, cheerful and successful lives.

Start Today… you have nothing to lose… but you have a life to win…

The first step towards success is taken when you refuse to be a captive of the environment in which you first find yourself. Remember that you become what we think about, and since you are thinking of your goal, you realize that soon it will be yours. In fact, it's really yours the moment you write it down and begin to think about it. **"Act as though it's impossible to fail".**

Successful people take decisive and immediate action; they make logical and informed decisions, and work outside the comfort zone. Success is the sum of small efforts, repeated day-in and day-out.

The difference between insanity and genius is measured only by success. No matter what your goal is, if you have kept the goal before you every day, you'll wonder and marvel at this new life you found. We become what we think about. Napoleon Hill. If you think positive you achieve positive results. If you think negative you lose. The secret to success is becoming bigger than our problems.

People who succeed have momentum, the more they succeed, the more they want to succeed, the more they find a way to succeed. Similarly, when someone is failing the tendency is to get on downward spiral that they can even become self-fulfilling prophecy. The road to success and the road to failure are almost the same. Your field of focus determines what you find in life.

"As You Plant –So you shall reap". Plant the seed into your mind, care for it, and work steadily towards your goal, it'll become a reality. Each must live off the fruits of our thoughts in the future; we are guided by our thoughts. We become what we think about.

Picture yourself as having achieved your goal and doing what you anticipated doing after having reached your goal. If you want to achieve excellence, you can get there today. As of this second, quit doing less-than-excellent work. You may only succeed if you desire succeeding; you may only fail if you do not mind failing. The moment you decide on a goal to work toward, you are immediately a successful person. Don't concern too much with how you are going to achieve your goal, leave that completely to greater power than yourself. Just know when you are heading to. The answers will come to you of their accord, at the right time. ***Start Today. You have nothing to lose. But you have the whole life to win.***

What simple action could you take today to produce a new momentum toward success in your life? The future belongs to those who prepare for it today. Often the difference between a successful person and a failure is not one has better abilities or ideas, but the courage that one must bet on one's ideas, to take a calculated risk - and to act.

Courage is resistance to fear, mastery of fear - not absence of fear. *Keep an eye on the goal and keep moving towards the target.* Only put off until tomorrow what you are willing to die having left undone. People often say that motivation doesn't last. Well, neither does bathing - that's why we recommend it daily. *The purpose of our life is to add value to the people of this generation and those to follow.*

Coming together is a beginning, keeping together is a progress and working together is success. Success is liking yourself, liking what you do, and liking how you do it. Nothing less will do. This includes the level of your achievements, the results you produce, the quality of your relationships, the state of your health and physical fitness, your income, your debts, your feelings—everything! Be responsible for your own actions.

Visualize the stepping stones that you will need to cross to achieve your goal, much like rungs on a ladder. And then ever strive to get your foot on the next rung. Constantly keep your eye on the goal, lest you lose sight of it and are side-tracked. Circumstances may happen that we didn't plan or envision. Don't let it deter you. For all I know these circumstances may just be another easier route for you to achieving your goal. *Ninety-nine percent of all failures come from people who have a habit of making excuses.* If *you* want to create the life of your dreams, then *you* are going to have to **take 100%.**

Success is the sum of small efforts repeated day in day out. Success is better understood and easily achieved with patience and perseverance. A successful person beliefs the future can be better than the present and has the power to realise it. A successful person is a winner; he never gives up neither quits.

To accomplish your goals there is no elevator to success you must take the stairs to climb to the top but once on top of the view is breath taking. We normally become stronger and bolder when we overcome challenges.

Successful life comes when you simply refuse to give up. Have goals that are so strong that obstacles and failure will act as a motivation. Be the creator of your own opportunities, don't let failure stop you. The best revenge of failure is massive success walk the extra mile and move mountains.

Work extra hard to achieve your dream. You are destined for greatness; just realise that your potential will haunt you if you don't give it your all.

Believing in your ability is the first secret to success. Believe you can do it, you deserve it and you will get it. If you don't build your dream someone will hire you to help them build their dreams. Successful people make decisions based on what they want to be.

A strong positive self-image is the best preparation for success. To be successful don't settle for average, success is hard work with persistence, perseverance, learning, studying, sacrifice and most of all have passion for what you are doing.

Never dream about success work hard towards it, your focus should be very intense. Be the game changer, positive habits with confidence are the foundation to success. Success is the ability to go from to failure to another without loss of enthusiasm. Keep moving and everything you have ever wanted in your life will be realised at the perfect time.

Work hard in silence and let success be your noise. Remember success isn't what you accomplish in life but what you inspire others to do. When you are successful in life you create an opportunity in people's life. Be an encourager life is full of critic's people who are negative or the "dream stealers". Life becomes limitless if you remain fearless.

The key to failure is to try and please everybody else. Success is doing what is right at the right way at the right time. You realise that you control your own destiny. Learn from failures and start all over again this time better. The key to happiness is success.

Some people dream of success while other wake up and achieve their life intentions by working hard. Refuse to be anything else but successful. If you love what you are doing you will be successful. Success is how high you bounce after you hit the rock bottom.

Take a percentage of your earnings and stick it in savings account, or better yet, invest it. Successful entrepreneurs know everything about their business even they don't do themselves but pay others to do it. Discipline is the key to success.

Successful people produce more leaders not followers. Successful people do what unsuccessful people are not willing to do don't wish it were easier, wish you were better.

Starting Point of Success

It is not what you look for that matters, it's what you seek.

Your unlimited power lies in your ability to control your thoughts. A confused mind works in the direction of sickness, poverty, lack and limitation rather than in the direction of abundance, health and success. If you want to make a permanent change, stop focusing on the size of your problems and start focusing on the size of you.

If we are not creating our lives the way we want them to be, we are creating from our unconscious. But since life is consciousness, the most important task we have is the development of the highest possible consciousness. We can do this by looking at the conditions of our lives and challenging our beliefs, even if our ego is threatened.

Whenever we want something in our lives, we must let go of anything that is between what we believe and what we want. Your life is important. It is important to you, and it is important to the rest of the people on this planet. I believe that every person on this planet arrived here with a mission.

If you will listen to your intuition your purpose or your mission will be revealed to you. In your heart, you know exactly what you want. And if you will listen to your intuition, it will tell you. Your mind will sell you out, but your intuition never will. Your intuition is your connection with the Ultimate Power. Learn to trust it.

People can control you through your mind, but they can never control you through your intuition. We imagine we will lose something by following our intuition.

Successful people are not perfectionist; they keep things simple and focus in making small and continuous improvements. They measure and track their progress. When you find a greater meaning, you find the courage to overcome your fear.

Success usually comes to those who are too busy to be looking for It. Success doesn't come and find you. You must go out and get it. What a mind can conceive and believe it can achieve. **Make success a Must!**

Success is measured by quality of service you render. All successful people serve, the greater the success, the greater the service. Wealth is created from service.

"Wealth, like happiness is never attained when sort after directly. It comes as a by-product of providing useful service.

Successful person maintains a positive attitude as they learn from mistakes, they spend time with the motivational people who uplift them not bring them down and maintain a balance in life. Success means freedom from worries, fears and frustrations.

Just because its stormy now doesn't mean you aren't headed for sunshine.

Success seems connected with action; successful people keep moving. They make mistakes but they don't quit. I might lose the battles, but will not lose my faith, nor the will to keep going with my God. Ambition is the path to success. Winners never quit and quitters never win. Success how high you bounce when you hit bottom. If it fails don't give up repeat again and again and each time it'll become more part of you until you will wonder if you could have lived any other way e.g. Henry Ford.

Always be yourself, express yourself, have faith in yourself, and do not go out and look for a successful personality and duplicate it. The starting point of all achievement is desire.

People who succeed have momentum. The more they succeed the more they find a way to succeed. When someone is failing, the tendency is to get on a downward spiral that can even become a self-fulfilling prophecy. *The formula for success is quite simple, "Double your rate of failure".*

Failure isn't the enemy of success, but a stepping stone towards success. We learn through mistakes. "Bravery means finding something more important than fear."

Courage without meaning is just recklessness. Brave people aren't fearless; they've simply found something that matters more to them than the fear they're facing. Say you're scared to start a business. Find a reason that has greater meaning than the fear: *Your family's future, your desire to make a difference, or your dream of a more fulfilling life.*

The price of success is hard work, dedication to the job at hand and the determination that we did our level best for either the positive and negative results. Don't wait to achieve your goals start it today. Do your Best and God will do the rest. The size of your success is measured by the strength for your desire, size of your dream; and how you handle disappointments along the way.

Success is not the result of making money, earning money is the result of success.

Success is the direct proportion to our service. Don't concern yourself with money, be of service, build, work, dream and Create. Don't aim for success if you want it, just do what you love and believe in, and you'll find that there is no limit to prosperity and abundance that will come to you.

Success is not the key to happiness; happiness is the key to success. If you love what you are doing, you'll be successful. Happiness is the joy of achievement and the thrill of creative effort. Success is not final, failure is not fatal, it is the courage to continue that counts.

Success is measured not so much by the position that one has reached in life as the obstacles which he has overcome. To succeed, your desire for success should be greater than your fear of failure.

The less you respond too rude, critical, argumentative people, the more peaceful your life will become. You were born to win, but to be a winner; you must plan to win, prepare to win and expect to win no matter the consequences. There are no regrets in life just lessons.

Success is a peace of mind which is direct result of self-satisfaction in knowing you did your best you can become. What is right is not always popular, and what is popular is not always right.

> ***Until you dig a hole, you plant a tree; you water it and make it survive, You haven't done a thing. You are just talking.*** Wangari Maathai Winner Nobel Price.

There will be no fruit bearing trees if you don't plant a seed. Same as there'll be no better future if you won't work hard on it.

The price for SUCCESS is dedication, hard work, and unremitting devotion to the things you want to see. Motivation is what gets you started and habit is what keeps you going.

> ***Decide upon your major definite purpose in life and then organize all your activities around it.***

Live this new way and the floodgate of abundance will open and pour over you more riches than you may have dreamed existed. MONEY! Yes, you'll will have it in abundance, you'll also find peace… you'll be in the wonderful minority who lead calm, cheerful successful lives.

Start today you have nothing to lose but have a life to win. The secret of success is to become bigger than all your problems. The foundation stones for a balanced success are honesty, character, integrity, faith, love and loyalty. Success isn't a destination it's a journey. You don't pay the price for success; you enjoy the benefits of success.

The size of your success is measured by the strength of your desire; size of your dream; and how to handle disappointed along the way. Success is a peace of mind which is direct result of self-satisfaction in knowing you did your best that you can become. Develop success from failures. Discouragement and failure are two of the surest stepping stones to success. If you genuinely want something, don't wait for it – teach yourself to be impatient. If you go there in your mind, it's only a matter of time before you go there in body.

You must see it; if you can see it, if you can perceive it, then you will find a way to get it. To succeed, you must be hungry; you must thirst for success. Once you know what your life purpose is, you can organize all your activities around it.

Everything you do should be an expression of your purpose.

If an activity doesn't fit that formula, you wouldn't work on it. Period. What's the "why" behind everything you do? Without purpose as the compass to guide you, your goals and action plans may not ultimately fulfil you.

You don't want to get to the top of the ladder only to find out you had it leaning up against the wrong wall. A goal properly set is halfway reached. If you want to reach a goal, you must 'see the reaching' in your own mind before you arrive at your goal. Remember that failure is an event, not a person. Yesterday ended last night. If you don't see yourself as a winner, then you cannot perform as a winner.

When obstacles arise, you change your direction to reach your goal; you do not change your decision to get there. You will get all you want in life if you help enough other people get what they want. Obstacles are necessary for success because in life, victory comes only after many struggles and countless defeats.

Below is some of the life changing keys to success that will position you to succeed, to be your best and to live the life of your dreams.

The key to success is to focus our conscious mind on things we desire not things we fear.

Success is getting what we want: -

1. **The no. of times I succeed is in direct proportion of the no. of times I fail and keep trying.**
   You have everything you need to build something far bigger than yourself.

2. Always do your best. Whatever you do give it 100%. We never must be perfect but let us give it our best shot. Do a little more each day then you can think of and eventually you will settle for enough.

Life is about making choices, make the most positive choice you can have, what you plant now you'll harvest later. Always do your best never give up on hope, be kind to yourself and follow your heart. Be happy, smile everyday give sunshine into your life and always be grateful for what life must offer. The best preparation for tomorrow is doing your best today. Always do your best from making the right choices and learning from the wrong ones.

Just do it, quit making excuses waiting for the right time you create the moment, waiting until you are older, richer, braver don't dream about it, hit the rod when it's still hot just do your level best and eventually you'll realize your dream.

There are no back roads to success; everyone must climb the same mountain.

Success is an Iceberg that people see. Underneath the surface, Persistence, Failure, Sacrifice, Good Habit, Handwork, and Dedication Our dreams are realized after a lot of persistence. THINK AND GROW RICH

The path to success: -

1. Ambition is the path to success. First know the path and the walk the path.
2. Persistence is the vehicle you arrive in.
3. If you want to succeed do not travel on the worn paths (*business as usual*) rather strike out new paths (*business unusual*).
4. Willingness to take risks is the path to success.
5. Taking a massive and determined action to follow your lead is a path to success. There is no elevator to success but to take the stairs.
6. Failure is the path to success. When you fall wake up wipe the dust and move on with commitment and determination.
7. Strong ideas closely held together are a path to success.
8. A journey of a thousand miles begins with a single step. The million-dollar path is a series of small steps joined together.
9. No one is born successful, to succeed in life one must have courage, determination and strength to overcome all obstacles put on their path on the road to success
10. The road to success is not a path you find but a trail you blaze.
11. The hardest times often lead to the greatest moment of your life day in, day out. We are what we do repeatedly. Excellence is as a result.

S	-	See your goal
U	-	Understand your obstacles
C	-	Create a positive mental picture
C	-	Clear your mind off self-doubt
E	-	Embrace the challenge
S	-	Stay on track
S	-	Show and prove to the world you can do it.

The strongest factor for success is self-esteem: -

Believing you can do it, believing you will do it, & believing you deserve it.

Success demands loyalty and responsibility! Are you loyal to your duties, do you faithfully complete the critical tasks that are requisite to your success? Are you faithful to your responsibilities, are you consistent? To succeeds, you must be loyal to your passion; you must give it your all. If you don't build your dreams, someone will hire you to help them build yours, so please stop chasing the money and start chasing the passion.

Try not to become a person of success, but rather try to become a person of value. You must have passion to succeed. If success is to be yours, it will be yours while you are following your passion. You won't succeed doing something you despise, you won't even succeed doing something that you like doing, and you will succeed when you do what you love what you're passionate about.

People often want something for nothing. They want to work for a year and be rich for a lifetime. But real change requires a lifestyle change. There is no shortcut; you can't cheat the system, in fact the more you cheat the system, the further away from your goals you get.

Success looks simple, but it's rather hard because it requires consistent and change of your lifestyle (your daily actions, thinking and habits i. e working hard, eating right focusing on your goals).

Note. Habits will take you further than your desires; desires can only take you so far.... Before you burn out, you must rely on the trail tracks of habit to get to your destination.

> *To get the results you want, you must "adopt a lifestyle", and otherwise you will end up chasing a mirage in the desert of life. The "mirage" is a shortcut to your goal and so you can run after it, but it's just a mirage, only to put yourself further into the desert.*

To produce success, you must have the roots of success; **you must change your lifestyle.** Decide today to live a life that produces the rewards you desire.

Decide to change your habits! Decide to change your thinking!

Decide to learn from all those who have succeeded, look for a mentor.

Success is not the strongest of the species that survive, or the most intelligent, but the one most responsive to change. Opportunities don't happen. You create them. The distance between insanity and genius is measured only by success.

People rarely succeed unless they have fun in what they are doing. Success does not consist in never making mistakes but in never making the same one a second time. To be successful you must accept all challenges that come your way. You can't just accept the ones you like.

Success is knowing your purpose in life, growing to reach your maximum potential, and sowing seeds that benefit others. The key to success is keeping company with people who uplift you. Great minds discuss ideas; Average minds discuss events and small minds, discuss people.

> **Stop waiting for the 'right time.' Success is a numbers game: the number of times you take a shot.**

You'll never create the perfect business plan, never find the perfect partners, the perfect market, the perfect location, but you can find the perfect time to start. That time is *now*. Choose your priorities. It is our choices that show what we truly are, for more than our abilities.

At every instant, every day, you are making a choice of how you spend your time. You have a limited amount of time, so time is a highly valuable currency. You certainly can't do everything that you consider doing or those others ask you to do.

You establish your real priorities in life by your choices, how you allocate your time. Whenever you spend time on some mindless activity or allocate time to meeting someone else's demands (they don't further your own life purpose) you have chosen your priorities wrongly.

Don't confuse leisure *"priorities that further your own life purpose"* time recreation activities like resting, reading or picnic /partying, which create balance in life by relieving stress, relaxing you making you happier and strengthening your connection with family and friends. With *"priorities unlikely to further your life* purpose" e.g. surfing the web, checking the email every few seconds, chatting online, watching TV, or video gaming etc.

Take the extra mile it's never crowded, people of excellence go the extra mile to do what is right. There are no limits only plateaus and must go beyond them to enjoy the view on top.

By going the extra mile lend better service than you are being paid for. If you are a sales person stop selling and start helping give a solution to the client not create profit and whatever you do if you apply wisdom, you'll eventually be successful.

Be a person of excellence and go the extra mile by doing what is right. There are no traffic jams along the extra mile. The brave man is not the one who's afraid but the one who conquers fear.

Only those who risk going too far can possibly find out how far they can go.

Let us move out of the comfort zone area and go farther, initially its difficult but after working extra harder and bear positive results that what's makes us great.

By going the extra mile today, I do what others don't do so that tomorrow I can achieve what others can't and will see you at the top.

Rules of Success are:

Break some rules- do the impossible, go the extra mile to achieve your goal. If you do not step forward, you'll always be stagnant.

1. Believing in yourself follow your heart it'll lead you there. If you do not go after what you want, you will never have it.
2. Don't be afraid to fail. failure is the starting point to success. Fear paralyzes people. Step out of the comfort zone. We learn from failures.
3. Ignore the negative people. You can't reach your full potential without haters. Keep company of those who uplift you.
4. Work like hell. Strength is developed from your struggles. When you go through hardships and don't give up the strength to move on is developed. Determination today leads to success tomorrow.
5. Give something back; we rise by lifting one another. Life is a gift and it offers us the privilege, opportunity and responsibility to give something back to the society and to becoming more. Everyone needs to be valued. ***Give to Inspire others to give.***

The key to success is keeping company with people who uplift you, whose presence calls forth your best.

To be successful you must accept all challenges that come your way. You can't just accept the ones you like.

Be content to act, and leave the talking to others. You may have to fight a battle more than once to win it.

> *"Today's pain is tomorrow's power. The more you suffer today, the stronger you are tomorrow."*

Self-pity is self-defeating. Tomorrow's success is based on today's discomfort. Plus, willpower is like a muscle: the more you exercise it, the stronger your will gets. And the easier it is to call on when dedication and persistence make all the difference. Be patient with yourself. Self-growth is tender; it's holy ground. There's no greater investment.

Many of life's failures are people who did not realize how close they were to success when they gave up. Successful and unsuccessful people do not vary greatly in their abilities. They vary in their desires to reach their potential

Successful people do what unsuccessful people are not willing to do. The price to success is dedication, hard work and unremitting devotion to the things you want to see happen.

Success is a peace of mind which is direct result of self-satisfaction in knowing you did the best you can do.

Our greatest fear should not be of failure but of succeeding at things in life that don't really matter.

Success does not consist in never making mistakes but in never making the same one a second time.

CHAPTER 7

Success and Failure

Success is failure turned inside out. I can accept failure; everyone fails at something. But I can't accept not trying

Success is walking from failure to failure with no loss of enthusiasm.

How can you succeed if you never try? How can you go to your grave knowing that you never tried? Don't go to your tomb empty. You may not know what paths will work best for you, the only way to discover the right path — is to try. Try and try, until you discover your difference. Try until you learn where you can be a success.

Success is not final; failure is not fatal. It is the ***courage*** *to* continue that counts.

The difference between a successful person and others is not lack of strength, not lack of knowledge but rather lack of willpower.

Success is about creating benefit for all and enjoying the process. If you focus on this and adopt this definition, success is yours, success is limitless. The difference between a successful person and others is not lack of strength, not lack of knowledge but rather lack of will.

To succeed your desire should be greater than your failure. Success is how high you bounce when you hit bottom. Let him who would enjoy a good future waste none of his present, live as if you were to die tomorrow and learn as if you were to live forever. Twenty years from now you will be more disappointed by the things you didn't do than the ones you did do. A successful man is the one who can lay a firm foundation with bricks others have thrown to him.

If success is to be yours, you can rest assured that you're going to have to work at it. To be the best, you must give your best; you must work harder than the rest. While people are resting, you must be working.

Success is a game, you must play hard, you must out-smart the competition, and you must put in the work. Always believe that if you put in the work, the results will come. "I don't know the key to success, but the key to failure is trying to please everyone."

Never fear failure, fear not trying, fear not giving your best, fear losing focus, but never fear failure. Failure is the path to success. Failure is the sign that you're headed in the right direction.

To succeed twice as fast, fail twice as much. Fail often, fail daily, and soon you will succeed. Never be afraid to fail. You can beat the statistics but if you stumble along your journey, brush yourself off and keep moving.

Success will come. There's a saying by the great businessman and inventor, that success is 10 percent inspiration and 90 percent perspiration.

While it's one thing to be an entrepreneur and come up with an idea, get funding and start a small business, it's another to achieve success with it. The statistics paint a challenging picture to do so as approximately 30 percent of new companies don't last longer than two years and almost 50 percent only last for five years. That's the hard part of starting new business: finding lasting success.

Success is not final, failure is not fatal; it is the courage to continue that counts.

Don't let failure overtake the determination to succeed. Success is the result of perfection, hard work, learning from failure, loyalty and persistence.

Failure is not the opposite of success; it is part of success. Failure is Success In progress. You won't become successful unless you encounter failure.

Failure is part of success, you pass through failure to succeed.

Let your failure be motivation to success. Failure is unfinished success. It is success if we learn from it.

Twenty years from now you will be more disappointed by the things you didn't do than by the ones you did do. So, throw off the bowlines. Sail away from the safe harbour. Catch the trade winds in your sails. Explore! Dream! Discover!"

If you want to make a permanent change, stop focusing on the size of your problems and start focusing on the size of you!

Develop success from failures.

1. Develop your life purpose definition by finding your values, your strengths, passion and your worldly needs. Follow your path, you become truly alive when you honour your calling. When you find your passion, and mission you eventually live your purpose by believing in your goals and you reach the stars to change the world.

2. A master mind alliance is when a group of individual minds are co-ordinated and function in harmony. The team working together with trust, enthusiasm, encouragement and motivate each other to achieve a definite common objective. A mastermind group think, share, inspire to lead other team members. You acquire all your desires in life when you help others achieve their desires. A real leader becomes great by his ability to empower other realise their achievements.

3. Go the extra-mile. There is no traffic by going the extra mile you attain anything you decide to do. Define yourself, follow your path, motivate yourself to overcome all handles along the path. If you are ready and willing miracles come in moments, it's never crowded along the extra mile.

4. Start believing that it will happen. Believe in yourself and your abilities, know that there is something greater than any obstacles. Believing is the strongest success weapon, believe it will work out, you'll see opportunities. Magic is all around you just must believe it.

5. Have a personal initiative. When your desires, determination and ambition are strong enough you will be able with push for to realise your objection. When you stay focused towards your goal every day is a chance to change your life.

6. Creativity takes courage. Every accomplishment start with a decision to try. Life is about creating yourself. By being creative you lose the fear of being on the wrong and learn to trust our talents. Creative is normally intelligence having fun.

7. The real secret of success is enthusiasm. Enthusiasm moves the world. When you plan to do, a thing be enthusiastic, put your soul into it, plan, be active, be energetic, be faithful, stamp your personality into it, be passionate about it and you'll accomplish your objective. When you put enthusiasm in everything you do success will be realised.

8. Think accurately: - focus on the possibilities and you will have more opportunities to realise your goals. You only have one life to live, believe in yourself, make yourself proud, take risks on what makes you feel good and do not allow negative vibes to way you down. Be positive, even if you triple and fall, wake up rub the dust off and move on. Remember the best view comes after the hardest climb.

9. Self-determination: - stay positive and focused, work hard be fearless in pursuit of our goals. If you truly believe in your dreams, there is no other force more powerful than the determination to succeed. Just believe you can and you will, stay determined either find

a way or create a way, difficulties mean going the extra mile eventually all that you have wished for will be realised.

10. Profit from adversity: - hardships often prepare ordinary people for extra ordinary destiny. In times of adversity that's when we discover our true self. You realise your inner strength when you overcome obstacles and achieve your success. *"Don't be broken by adversities Break Records*

Must-Read Success Lessons

1. **The Mind-**
Have a dream with a plan? Help converting the dream into a vision with a mission. If you go there in your mind, it's only a matter of time before you go there in body. You must see it; if you can see it, if you can perceive it, then you will find a way to get it. To succeed, you must be hungry; you must thirst for success.

2. **Look for opportunities: -**
Assess the market, look for your strengths and weaknesses, deal with problems by looking for solutions. If you're trying to achieve, there should be no road blocks. But obstacles don't have to stop you.
Obstacles are what prepare you for success. If you run into a wall, don't turn around and give up. Figure out how to climb it, go through it, or work around it. Obstacles aren't a bad thing; they're the training grounds to success.

3. **Perspective –**
Believe in yourself. Success begins through believing in what you can do. To succeed you must turn negative situations into positive ones.
You must see the positive; you must become positive, to experience success. Being positive, it's the only way up the ladder of success.

4. **Loyalty and Responsibility:**
Success demands loyalty and responsibility. Be patient, nothing happens overnight. Accept failure and be patient. Failure is part of journey towards success. To succeed you must be consistent, faithful to your responsibilities, you must be loyal to your passion; and you must give it your all.

5. **Learn from Your Failures: -**
Failure is a chance to learn, simply the opportunity to begin again, this time intelligently. Failure is unfinished success, it's part of life, if you don't fail you don't learn, if you don't learn you'll never change.

6. **Make It Happen: -**

Success is no accident. It is hard work, perseverance, learning studying and most of all love what you are doing. To succeed, you're going to have to roll up your sleeves, put your head down, and make it happen at all costs. Life is a succession of lessons which must be lived and understood.

To make your dream come true devote yourself to an idea, go make it happen, struggle on it, overcome your fear and smile, stay positive, work hard and you'll make it happen.

7. **Passion –**

The only way to do great work is to love what you do. Choose a job you love and you'll never have to work a day in your life.

You must have passion to succeed. If success is to be yours, it will be yours while you are following your passion hard work and sacrifice and above all don't let anyone limit your dreams. Make your passion your pay check.

In the end, passion, persistence and hard works beats out the natural talent.

8. **Try:**

To succeed you must try hard enough, remember there is nothing that is worth that comes the easy way.

It is not how hard you try, but how well you'll succeed by trying harder.

Striving for success without hard work is like trying to harvest where you have not planted.

Try and try, until you discover your difference. Try until you learn where you can be a success. No matter how hard keep trying.

9. **Work**

Dream Big, work hard. Be a goal setter and work hard towards achieving it. Be work in progress. If the success is to be yours, you can be assured that you must work hard to achieve your goals.

To excel you must go the extra mile. Be of service, give your best, put extra work to outsmart the competition. When you become successful the result will be prosperity and abundance. You must earn money by providing services or selling products. You must work first to be successful. Set a definite goal for every action done if positive the outcome will yield positive results. Be the person you want to become. Success is a result you earn money after the work output. Start today to be successful by focusing all your energy on the goal. When you move out of the comfort zone, you will achieve all that you have worked for. Work hard in silence let success be your noise.

10. **Failure**

Failure is the stepping stone to success. Be positive don't fear failure. Learn from your past failures to create a successful tomorrow. When you are persistence you will be successful.

Make failure be an opportunity for a new beginning. Make failure a lesson, use the experience to come back more stronger and bold. You only fail if you stop trying. Fall down several times and rise rub the dust and move on.

Let us learn from the failures we have experienced in life; don't quit. Remember there is a secret of opportunity that is inside every failure. Every failure is a lesson. Those who dare to fail miserably can achieve greatly. Failure makes your story extra ordinary.

Failure is nothing more than a chance to revise your strategy. Fail your way to succeed. We learn from failures not success. You become successful when you can handle setbacks. When you are persistence you become successful. Winners were once failures but persisted until they succeeded. Remember failure is not fatal but unfinished success.

11. **Don't wait for the right moment create the right moment.**

We should have courage to take risks and move towards something we anxiously want. We should never hold back from possibilities opportunities, discovery and the world adventures.

Waiting for the right moment or the right partner is often a mistake since life is too short and we will run out of time eventually and life will always get on the way if we must wait for the right moment.

Just create right the perfect business plan, never find the perfect partners, the perfect market, the perfect location, but you can find the perfect time to start. That time is *now*. Just make time for the important things you want to accomplish.

Acting will result to a more fulfilled and exciting life. Even in failure you are learning, by taking risks you'll be better prepared in future. From repeated failures, you perfect your act's and once you are skilled you eventually live your fulfilled life to the fullest.

Revisit your purpose, jump at the right moment and create a life changing experience.

CHAPTER 8

The Power of Gratitude

Gratitude makes sense of our past, brings peace to today, and creates a vision for tomorrow.

Starting a day with gratitude can create the most wonderful day.

When you rise in the morning, think of what a precious privilege is to be alive, to breathe, to think, to enjoy, and to love.

Inner peace is choices make that choice today. Though no one can go back and make a brand-new start, anyone can start from now and make a brand-new ending. Don't wish it were easier; wish you were better. With gratitude, all the life appears to be a blessing, without gratitude all of life is perceived as a burden.

At any moment, some things are going well, while others are not going as we would choose. Being grateful for the blessings you get in your life, including the life lessons that come from setbacks; sets your mind for positive thinking and for enjoying a positive life.

Count your Blessings: - Gratitude unlocks the fullness of life:

It turns what we have into enough, and more. It turns denial into acceptance, chaos into order, and confusion into clarity. It turns a meal into a feast, a house into a home, a stranger into a friend.

The way of happiness is **"Zero-Based Gratitude"**.

Each day be grateful for what you have, independent of yesterday and of other people. Be grateful for all your life. Be grateful for the miracle of being you. Be grateful you are alive. Be grateful that you have food and shelter.

Be grateful of the beauty of the world, even if you are blind and homeless.

Be grateful and happy when life goes well, and avoid anger and resentment when life is not fair. You can always find things for which you can be grateful of.

There are only two ways to live your life. One as though nothing is a miracle, the other as though everything is a miracle. A grateful mind is a great mind which eventually attracts itself great things. To live a life fulfilled reflects on the things you have with gratitude. Focus on what you have, you'll be happy and you'll feel good about yourself, not miserable on what you don't have.

When we focus on what is available we will feel good about ourselves and experience happiness and we won't complain for what we lack.

Visualize a bright future; set your mind for positive thinking and enjoy living a positive, happy and prosperous life. Let us be grateful for the people who make us happy. They are charming gardeners who make our souls blossom. Be grateful not only for others but for yourself.

Develop an attitude of gratitude and trust your purpose. The more grateful you are the more present you become; the smallest thanks are always worth more than you realise. Being grateful, feeling good about yourself is the foundation of abundance. If you concentrate on finding whatever is good in every situation, your life will be filled with gratitude a feeling that nurtures your soul.

The struggle ends when gratitude begins when you start trusting yourself, trusting your purpose, trusting your goals, trusting your abilities and trusting your inherent worth as a person. Gratitude is a powerful process for shifting your energy and bringing more of what you want in life. Develop an attitude of gratitude and trust your purpose.

Appreciating the little you have now is the foundation to gratitude. The greatest source of happiness is the ability to be grateful always.

Gratitude is a muscle, the more you use it, the stronger it grows. Find blessings in everything by being grateful. Celebrate each special day and with gratitude life becomes rich.

The essence of all beautiful art, all great art is gratitude. Begin each day with gratitude and watch your life blossom. When I started counting my blessing, my whole life turned around. Be thankful for what you have; you'll end up having more. If you concentrate on what you don't have, you will never, ever have enough.

Gratitude makes sense for our past, brings peace for today, and creates a vision for tomorrow.

Gratitude changes everything, gratitude is the is the open door to abundance.

The struggle ends when gratitude begin Gratitude opens the door to power, the wisdom, the creativity of the universe. The real gift of gratitude is that the more grateful you are, the more present you become. The more you are in a state of gratitude, the more you'll attract things to be grateful for.

Develop an **"attitude of gratitude"** toward whatever you have now and watch how it will begin to grow and increase. He who can give thanks for little will always find he has enough. Be grateful for what you already have and you will attract more **Good Things**.

To speak gratitude is courteous and pleasant, to enact gratitude is generous and noble, but to reach gratitude is to touch heaven. No one who achieves success does so without acknowledge the help of others. The wise and confident acknowledge this with gratitude.

When you rise in the morning, give thanks for the light, for the life and for your strength. Give thanks for the food and for the joy of living. If you see no reason to give thanks, the fault lies in yourself.

As we express our gratitude, we must never forget that the highest appreciation is not to utter words but to live by them.

> *I write about the power of trying, because I want to be okay with failing, I write about generosity because I battle selfishness, I write about joy because I have known sorrow. I write about faith because I lost mine, and I know what it is to be broken and in need of redemption.*

> *I write about gratitude because I am thankful for all of it.* Thankfulness is the beginning of gratitude; gratitude is the completion of thankfulness. Thankfulness consists merely of words; gratitude is shown by action. Gratitude is a mark of noble soul and a refined character. We like to be in the company of people who are grateful. Gratitude is absolutely the way to bring more into your life.

> *Acknowledging the good that you already have in your life is the foundation for all abundance.*

> *The Essence of all beautiful art, all great art, is gratitude. Thankfulness creates gratitude which generates contentment hence causing a lot of peace and tranquillity.*

The Secret

ASK! BELIEVE! RECEIVE
The greatest Secret is the Law of Attraction

Whatever the mind can conceive, it can achieve. There is no such thing as a hopeless situation. Every single circumstance in life can change.

Turn the positive thoughts to the universe and you will realise the magic and miracles happening. Whatever you wish and conceive that is what you receive; positive mind attracts positive and negative mind will realise negativity.

You are what you think. Thoughts becomes things. What you think is what you create. Life is happening to you and you are creating it. What you feel and attract and whatever you imagine you become. To be happy you must have positive thoughts.

The secret is discovering the unknown. Take the first step in faith. You do not have to see the whole staircase just take the first step when you reach the top the view is worth the effort.

Believe it can be done, think about it, talk and act as though you have received it.

Your thoughts are the seeds, think positive and yield positive results, you harvest the seeds you plant.

To attract money focus on wealth. I wanted to be an author, I started writing notes, then blogs and eventually I wrote my book.

The key is your thoughts and feelings and remember you are holding the key of your life in your hands. With the Law of Attraction, you can create anything that you want to become by eliminating all the doubts with full expectations and you will receive all that you have ever wished to have. All that we are is because of our own thoughts. You create your own universe as you go along.

The secret of success in life is a man to be ready for his opportunity when it comes. Imagination is everything. It is the preview of life's coming attraction.

Whatever a man can conceive and believe it can be achieved. If you dream it you can realise it. The only person you are destined to become is the person you decide to be. Self-control is strength. Right thought is mastery and calmness is power.

A person becomes limited only by the thoughts he chooses to be. Life is always what you make of it.

The magic is believing in yourself and what you believe you can be, if you have faith you can become. You become what you think about.

You are a living magnet, you attract wealth, health, love and joy in your life. You become a living magnet and what you want to become the universe will manifest.

Choose your thoughts carefully, you are the masterpiece of your live. You create your own universe. Your thought become things when you see things that you want they are already yours. By writing this book I am *"Flying My Dreams Today"*.

Live your dreams, if you dream it you can do it. You are the one who calls the Law of Attraction into action and you do it through your thoughts. You become what you think about most of the time.

Printed in the United States
By Bookmasters